# Los celos / Dealing with Jealousy

Santana Hunt
Traducido por Eida de la Vega

Gareth Stevens
PUBLISHING

conceptos
básicos

Todos sobresalimos en
cosas diferentes.

---------------------------------

We are all good
at different things.

2

Tal vez tu hermana corre rápido. Quizás tu amigo dibuja bien.

---

Your sister might be a fast runner.
Your friend might be good at drawing.

5

A veces, nos sentimos celosos de los talentos de otros.

----------------------------------------

Other people's talents sometimes make us jealous.

7

Sentimos celos por las cosas que otros tienen, y nosotros no.

----------------------------------

We feel jealous about things another person has that we do not.

8

Los celos son un
sentimiento de enojo
y malestar.

----------------------------------------

Jealousy is an angry
or upset feeling.

Es posible que te den ganas de pelear con la persona de quien tienes celos.

-----------------------------------

We might want to fight with the person we are jealous of.

12

13

Podemos decir cosas crueles de ellas.

---

We might say mean things about them.

14

15

A veces, sentir celos
¡es normal!

------------------------------

It is okay to feel jealous.
It is normal!

16

17

Hablar o escribir acerca de cómo te sientes puede ayudarte a expresar tus sentimientos.

---------------------------------

Talking or writing about how you feel can help get your feelings out.

18

Piensa en todas las cosas
que *tú* sabes hacer bien.
¡Seguro que son muchas!

--------------------------------

Think about all the things
*you* are good at.
You have nice things, too.

No te compares con otros. ¡Tú también eres especial!

----------------------------------

Do not compare yourself to others. You are special, too!

Please visit our website, www.garethstevens.com. For a free color catalog of all our high-quality books, call toll free 1-800-542-2595 or fax 1-877-542-2596.

Library of Congress Cataloging-in-Publication Data

Hunt, Santana.
Dealing with jealousy = Los celos / by Santana Hunt.
p. cm. — (Minding our manners = Cuida tus modales)
Parallel title: Cuida tus modales.
In English and Spanish.
Includes index.
ISBN 978-1-4824-1734-0 (library binding)
1. Jealousy — Juvenile literature. I. Title.
BJ1535.J4 H86 2015
152.4—d23

First Edition

Published in 2015 by
**Gareth Stevens Publishing**
111 East 14th Street, Suite 349
New York, NY 10003

Copyright © 2015 Gareth Stevens Publishing

Designer: Andrea Davison-Bartolotta
Editor: Kristen Rajczak
Spanish Translation: Eida de la Vega

Photo credits: Cover, p. 1 (main) Gladskikh Tatiana/Shutterstock.com; cover, back cover, p. 1 (blue background) Eky Studio/Shutterstock.com; p. 3 petrograd99/iStock/Thinkstock; p. 5 (main) Serega K Photo and Video/Shutterstock.com; p. 5 (inset) 2xSamara.com/Shutterstock.com; p. 7 Robert Mandel/iStock/Thinkstock; p. 9 Stephan Hoeck/Getty Images; p. 11 imtmphoto/iStock/Thinkstock; p. 13 Martin Novak/Shutterstock.com; p. 15 llike/Shutterstock.com; p. 17 Pressmaster/Shutterstock.com; p. 19 Jupiterimages/Stockbyte/Thinkstock; p. 21 Patrick Foto/Shutterstock.com; p. 23 monkeybussinessimages/iStock/Thinkstock.

Printed in the United States of America

CPSIA compliance information: Batch #CW15GS: For further information contact Gareth Stevens, New York, New York at 1-800-542-2595.